HORIZON

SAYALI WAGLE

I dedicate this book to my grandparents who have always looked at the brighter side of life in the darkest times and have taught me to do the same.

To Aaji and Aajoba!

Contents

Contents

Preface

This book is a collection of my understanding of the similarities between human life and nature. God's creations on earth and beyond are not only beautiful but also hold something for each one of us. Everything in this book is about the little happenings on either side of the Horizon.

This book is my journey from capturing these little things on the camera to extracting lessons from them.

This is my first attempt at writing a book. Hence, I preferred to keep it short, yet meaningful.

Hope you enjoy this read!

1. Home

I said I was lost
when the storm turned everything
upside down.
I sat by the river,
next to a young boy
who barely noticed me.
He made little ripples
in the otherwise calm river water.
He giggled as he tricked the fishes
by pushing them away.
"Why don't you let them swim?"
I popped a casual question
to break the unbearable silence.
He looked at me sternly
and said in a very obvious tone,
"As if they'll get lost
in the water!"
"But…
you're confusing them
by changing their direction."
He sighed a little
and spoke again,

"It is their home.
They know how to go back.
Even if a storm erupts,
they're still inside their home!"
I said I was lost
when the storm turned everything upside down
until the world
became my home.

2. Moonrise

The two adjacent stages were lit,

and everything else blacked out.

The performances were flawless.

The two actors met backstage

after watching their respective audiences leave.

Both seemed content.

Curious,

one of them asked the other,

"I just performed

in front of a large audience.

Every single ticket was sold.

You could barely fill the first row.

What are you smiling for?"

The other grinned

as he looked out of the window.

The world gathered

on one end,

eagerly awaiting the

sunset.

But the moon stepped in

for the little girl waiting

for moonrise.

3. Reflect

Every feature of the tree glowed
as the little dew drops gathered.
Every passerby stopped
to admire the beauty added
to the leaves and flowers.
The leaves and flowers
became the medium
for the dew drops to shine.
The dew drops repaid their debt
by reflecting their colour to the world.

4. Bloom

The rich and the poor
lived alongside;
the difference
breaking them into
two groups of adversity.
Neither surpassed the other in life
but bloomed
in their own different ways,
in their own different worlds;
like the garden around the Roses
and the mud around the Lotus.
The Rose refused to grow
alongside the Lotus.
That doesn't stop the Lotus
from blooming.

5. Alike

They kept counting
the twinkling stars.
Being the only one
shining the brightest
as the dark sky agreed
to be the canvas,
the magnificent moon
waited to be adored.
He said to a little star,
"You're all the same.
Some of you,
trying your best
to shine brighter.
But can you ever be the moon?"
"Yes, we're all alike.
And we'll never be the moon.
But would you believe me if I said
that we're happy being the stars?"
The moon smiled,
"I am the only one,
you're many.
Why would you not want to be the moon?"

The star sparkled a little more as it said,
"Because,
we're many,
you are alone."

6. Mourn

The roots went deeper
as the plant decided
to grow away from the soil.
It taught its branches, leaves, and flowers
to do the same.
The soil silently let the roots
tighten their grasp
on its tiny grains
and let the plant take
anything that was offered
to the soil.
Years went by
and the soil wished and waited
for at least one leaf
or branch
to question their distance
but in vain.
The plant became a tree
and the distance kept growing
until the highest branch and the leaves it held,
did not know
of the soil's existence.

A day finally came
when the oldest leaf touched the soil.
The tree let it go.
The soil
mourned its death.

7. Different

Seeds of the same fruit,
but planted at different times.
One was still a sapling,
planted years later,
while the other touched the skies.
The little one kept growing
bit by bit,
hoping to meet the tree someday.
The tree, out of pride,
refused to crouch.
The sapling wondered
whether they were the same,
born out of seeds
that lived in the same fruit,
though sowed at different times.
They talked only to the ones
who managed to reach them.
The seed did not matter,
the growth did.
Same, yet different,
the sapling knew it had to grow enough
to be able to meet the trees.

8. Desert

"There's no one
to adore you here,
no one to even look at you.
Why do you still shine here
when you know
that you'll not be seen?"
the desert asked the Moon
with a heavy heart.
"The Sun shines upon you
so that the people
find their way out.
But you, my dear,
endure the burns
that accompany his presence.
It's true
that no one watches me here, in this vast land.
But you deserve the cool
after you've suffered
the burns.
You deserve a starry night
once you're done
with the day."

9. Pride

Pride was soaring high
but couldn't withstand
the tall tree.
Higher it began to soar,
higher than the tallest tree.
But crashed,
like a cloud
on a mountain
that stood in the way
of its flaunting.
Finally,
pride soared higher
than it ever had.
High enough to look down
upon the world beneath.
So sure it was
to remain untouched
by anything or anyone.
Just then,
another cloud passed by
and their mere touch
was enough

to drag both down.
Just like a cloud
floating in the skies,
pride could withstand anything
but see another cloud
filled with pride.

10. Flourish

The flowers
were all that the tall, flourished tree could ask for.
Adorned in all possible colours,
it would make heads turn
and the feet trace their path
back to them.
One day,
a red leaf shone
on a flowerless tree.
Flourishing had
a different meaning thenceforth.

11. Flaws

The Sun kept burning all day
to keep the world going.
He kept burning
till the moon found its way.
No one noticed the burns.
The Sun took a break
and set early one day.
All that the world wondered
was whether he shone
more than the rest
to hide his flaws.

12. Storm

The sand enjoys
the soothing waves
as the little grains sway
with every splash.
The water tries
to get to know its every grain
by entering the shore
not at once
but bit by bit.
The sand gives in
without entering the sea.
To her,
the mere touch of the droplets
feels like
she knows the sea
better each day,
with each wave
that touches her
and goes back home.
She gives in
until it is too late
to have realized

that the sea gets to know
the nearest obstacle
before the storm
engulfs the world beyond.

13. Clean

Like a newborn child
opening its eyes to the world,
too fragile and young
for any virtues or sins to be weighed,
the snow was clean and white.
Adored by many
as long as it was bright.
Like a growing child,
it gradually saw the world
and the snow lost its charm.
The world blamed it
for not being what it used to be.
Like the newborn child,
the snow,
too,
was clean and bright
until a thousand people
stepped on it.

14. Destination

15. Seen

The shell loved the waters
and the sea pulled it in,
years ago.
With every wave
it went along;
sometimes
floating on the surface,
sometimes
hiding in its depths.
Years later,
it was thrown out on the shore.
It was thrown out
by the sea
that it had started calling
"home".
It lay almost lifeless
on the grainy sand
as the waves managed to push it farther.
Just when it feared
that it'd lose itself
in the heaps of sand,
a bunch of people gathered around it.

It realized
that it was only on the shore
where it would've been noticed.

16. Grow

You plant a seed
and keep looking at it every day
waiting to see every step of its growth.
Your joy is unexplainable
when you see it making its way
and peeping out of the earth
into a whole new world that welcomes it
with open arms.
You dream about the leaves
that will grow,
the first bud
that it'll bear
and how you'll witness it
blooming into a flower.
You feel like the most capable person on earth
who knows what your little sapling needs.
Just then
you see another plant
making its way out through the soil.
A seed of a fruit, that someone might have thrown out of their
balcony
and no one ever knew.

A seed, which the gardener
unknowingly pressed under his feet.
The one
whose existence was known
only to itself and the earth.
The one who, thus,
was never watered.
Making its way,
just like the one you cared for.
Absorbing the water that you poured over yours
as it spread all over the soil
and reached an unintentionally planted seed.
Not knowing that,
it thanked you with all its heart for taking good care;
for it never knew what it is like
to be taken care of;
to be watered.
It grows.
It grows tall enough to surpass you.
You collect its fruits in a basket
knowing that its existence
never made a difference to you.
Yet, it happily gives away its fruits to you,
not knowing
that it is an orphan;
that it was never taken care of.

17. Attend

A thousand drops came together
to quench the thirst of the living.
Relieved,
everyone pulled their chairs
to sit back after a long wait.
The plants now had a provider.
Startled
by the young boy running towards the plant,
everyone got back on their toes.
He gave half a glass of water
to the dried-up soil
and sprinkled some on the leaves.
"The rain is trying its best to be the giver," he said.
"But when they're naive
and under your shelter,
they will wait to be watered and attended to
by you."

18. Envy

The leaves envied the flowers.
Every passerby stopped
to look at the beauty,
smell it
and sometimes,
even give it a place on their canvas.
The women's hair tied in a bun,
the pendant of a delicate necklace,
the design on the clothes;
the flowers made their way
everywhere.
The leaves envied the flowers
until they saw
all the beauty
being plucked.

19. Help

Growing up,
the creeper held on to anything
that it found itself closer to.
The other plants laughed at it
as they grew independently.
The creeper grew;
slowly
and cautiously.
It did not give in
to the pressure.
It didn't try to leave
its support.
It beautified even the other plants
and the walls around.
It had dared
to accept
that it needed
help.

20. Clouds

Saving each drop of tear
like a treasure,
the cloud piles up his grief.
Like a grown-up,
trying to show how happy life is,
he floats,
far, far away.
He floats
as if he has never known grief.
He has many co-travelers on this journey
who ask him to let go.
Let go of the weight he carries.
They know
that they'll all have to let go someday.
Knowing that their grief
is why they are alive.

21. Spring

The spring was born
next to a large waterfall.
Always wondered
why it had to exist.
One day
it said it aloud,
"It's pitiful enough that I exist.
But why add to it
by putting me next to the waterfall?
Why flaunt its greatness
in front of a spring?"
A little voice heard
and replied to its worry,
"God was worried
we'll die
when a young little boy planted us here.
The waterfall,
however great,
by no means, could reach us little saplings.
You exist
so that we can!"

22. Wave

The wave rises high.
Higher than any other wave had.
Higher than it ever managed to rise.
Every person stood
with their eyebrows raised
as the wave seemed to touch
the sky.
It gradually descended
as it gulped down a life.
However high it rose,
when taking an innocent life,
it had stooped
to its lowest.

23. Whole

The ocean smiled
as the stars twinkled
right above him.
People gathered
to feel the sky closer to them.
The ocean said
to the stars,
"Your beauty
is what people see.
They stand by my side
and look up
only to be mesmerized by you.
I have nothing
that is worthy of admiration.
I have no purpose."
A star twinkled,
lesser than the other,
"I am not the brightest.
Many a time,
I'm not even noticed.
But,
for once,

*imagine the sky
with only the brightest stars.
They're not enough.
You, my friend,
are not a star.
But if it was not for you,
how would the world
define depth?"*

24. Close

The young girl full of dreams,
brave enough to sit by the window
and look at the eagle in the eye, spoke to him,
"I wish I could fly high like you.
And maybe look at the clouds.
Maybe be one amongst them.
What is it like, up there? How does it look?
How does it feel to be at the top of the world?"
The eagle took a step back,
his grip on the window pane still strong,
"It's pretty, young lady! It's pretty up there.
The planet is one whole.
Not what it is like from land.
Towns, cities, countries, race, religion - all of them look alike
from the world above.
The trees, wind, and oceans
rule the world from up there.
The earth looks calm;
as if she has no suffering, no fear,
as if she has never been a victim."
The young girl took a step closer
as if meaning to whisper to him,

"Then why are you here, my friend?
Why don't you go and see the world
from where it looks as it should?"
"Because, I don't want to miss the details.
It's a perfect world from where I see it.
I see it just the way you see the sky above
and yet would want to fly high to be closer.
The little things,
good and bad,
are what we go closer to.
The details,
of the gigantic earth or a tiny person with a thousand little
thoughts,
is what we go closer for."

25. Horizon

A thin line glowed,
marking the end
of the earth.
As beautiful as it looked,
it marked the end
of the beautiful sea.
But,
that is where
the Sun set.
That is where
the sky stepped in.
That surely is
where something beautiful
ended,
but
for another beautiful
beginning.

Link to the Blog: https://sayaliii.wordpress.com/author/sayaliii/

Write to me on: write.sayali@gmail.com

* 9 7 9 8 8 8 7 7 2 4 3 6 2 *